LITTLE QUICK FIX:

FIND THE THEME IN YOUR DATA

#LittleQuickFix

Sara Miller McCune founded SAGE Publishing in 1965 to support the dissemination of usable knowledge and educate a global community. SAGE publishes more than 1000 journals and over 800 new books each year, spanning a wide range of subject areas. Our growing selection of library products includes archives, data, case studies and video. SAGE remains majority owned by our founder and after her lifetime will become owned by a charitable trust that secures the company's continued independence.

Los Angeles | London | New Delhi | Singapore | Washington DC | Melbourne

LITTLE QUICK FIX:

FIND THE THEME IN YOUR DATA

Robert Thomas

SAGE

Los Angeles | London | New Delhi
Singapore | Washington DC | Melbourne

Los Angeles | London | New Delhi
Singapore | Washington DC | Melbourne

Sage Publications Ltd
1 Oliver's Yard
55 City Road
London EC1Y 1SP

Sage Publications Inc.
2455 Teller Road
Thousand Oaks, California 91320

Sage Publications India Pvt Ltd
B 1/I 1 Mohan Cooperative Industrial Area
Mathura Road
New Delhi 110 044

Sage Publications Asia-Pacific Pte Ltd
3 Church street
#10-04 Samsung hub
Singapore 049483

First published 2019

Editor: Alysha Owen
Editorial assistant: Lauren Jacobs
Production editor: Tanya Szwarnowska
Marketing manager: Ben Griffin-Sherwood
Cover design: Lisa Harper-Wells
Typeset by: C&M Digitals (P) Ltd, Chennai, India
printed in the UK

Library of Congress Control Number: 2019939804

British Library cataloguing in publication data

A catalogue record for this book is available from the British Library.

ISBN 978-1-5297-0124-1

Contents

Everything in this book!

Section 1 Finding a theme is at the heart of qualitative research and brings together smaller categories or ideas that represent significant trends in your qualitative data.

Section 2 The first thing to do when starting to look for themes is to organize your data and engage with it. You must develop a relationship with your data through transcription.

Section 3 Once you've transcribed your data you can start to analyse it initially through a robust reading strategy. Through reading you'll begin to familiarize yourself with what might be contained within your data.

Section 4 You will need to understand what coding and codes are before you begin a deeper analysis. Codes are the building blocks of your final themes.

Section 5 Now you can begin coding properly. Codes represent the researcher's first attempts to make sense of their data, so it's important to know what to look for.

Section 6 Next turn your codes into categories. To begin to form categories, compare all your codes to see if there are relationships between them that might be summed up by a larger category.

Section 7 Once you've developed your categories you can start to develop themes. Themes are built on significant and repeated ideas that have been established in your categories. Themes help you answer your research questions, but they need verification.

Section 8 Constructing your themes is sequential but also a very personal process. So, to ensure your themes are relevant, meaningful and representative, it is important that you get your themes and your work overall verified.

Finding a theme is at the heart of qualitative research

Section 1

Q

What is a theme?

A

Themes should be thought of as the main issues that emerge from a systematic process of data analysis beginning with transcription, coding and categorization.

Themes represent major repeating ideas in the data

A theme captures codes and categories that have similar meanings and unifies them under a significant heading, or a 'theme'. Themes help us then to understand fully what's been revealed by our participants in the data collection process and help present our analytical process more clearly. The good news is that you will decide what your themes are, as you will have analysed your own transcripts.

WHAT TYPE OF DATA GENERATES THEMES?

Any qualitative data collection method will generate what we call textual data. **Textual data is data taken from what people have said, and we use what people have said as evidence to support our research questions.** So, if you're engaging in any of the following, you're going to generate textual data:

1 Interviews (both structured and unstructured)

2 Focus groups (traditional, online and virtual)

3 Elite interviews

4 Event diaries

5 Ethnography

IS IT A JOURNEY OF DISCOVERY?

Very much so! **The data you'll have collected will be unique and what will be contained within it will also be unique.** It will have come from multiple individuals, multiple perspectives, and will provide multiple answers that will represent their experiences, ideas and feelings.

Your themes will be contained within your collected data. You'll find them through analysis; they're just waiting to be discovered in what your participants have said.

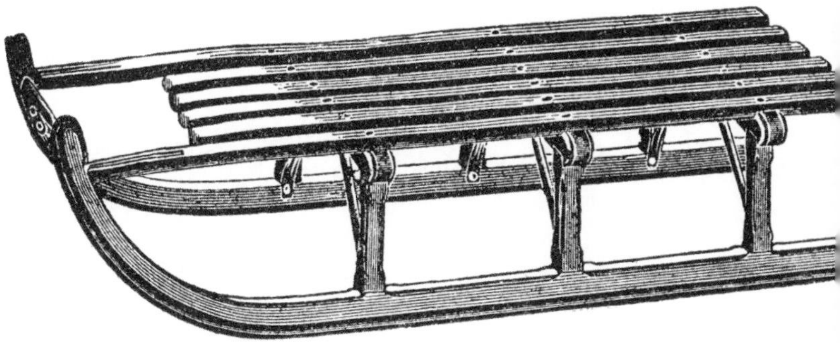

SO, MY FINAL THEMES WILL BE BASED ONLY ON MY DATA?

This is an important question, and the answer is yes. But this is dependent on your approach to research, so there are two ways that themes might develop:

Inductive approach – themes generated inductively stem from an analysis of what your participants have said. This approach doesn't rely on existing theory to define its themes and is applied when theory-building.

Deductive approach – themes generated deductively stem from using pre-existing knowledge, pre-existing thought, and pre-existing terms. This approach is applied when the researcher is looking to test or support current theory.

WILL I UNCOVER DIFFERENT TYPES OF THEMES?

You'll potentially discover several major or 'meta-themes' and several minor or 'sub-themes'. The differences are simple:

Meta-theme – this is significant theme that captures important, noteworthy, reoccurring and crucial elements within your data that clearly and identifiably answer your research question.

Sub-theme – this is a minor theme that has relevance in relation to answering your research question; it is of interest, but ultimately isn't as strong as a meta-theme. These should be used sparingly, unless they add to the answer.

HOW CAN I ENSURE I GET CREDIBLE THEMES?

We get themes through our data, so it's worth recalling that we need to have the following in place to ensure we get good data:

- [ ] You know your research question
- [ ] Your questioning framework covers your research question
- [ ] You've piloted your questions and questioning framework for clarity (essential)
- [ ] You've practised your skills as a moderator (we don't want bias)
- [ ] You've recruited well (participants should be able to answer your questions)
- [ ] You've captured your participants' biographical data
- [ ] Your participants know what they need to consider and why they're involved
- [ ] You have recording equipment (vital)
- [ ] Make notes during the actual recording, this will help capture your thoughts

CHECKPOINT

FILL IN THE MISSING WORDS

A .... should capture the major ideas and main issues that .... from the .... of your .... Themes will be generated by the answers your .... have already provided and you'll discover them through analysis of those answers. Analysis will begin by creating accurate .... of what has been, and this will create .... Once you've done that, you'll begin the .... process and then move onto .... Through this process, regardless of whether your approach is .... or .... you'll discover .... and potentially .... that will allow you to fully answer your ....

Categorization
Research question
Inductive
Analysis
Meta-themes
Transcriptions
Textual data
Qualitative data
Coding
Sub-themes
Participants
Deductive
Theme
Emerge

ANSWERS

CHECKPOINT

A theme should capture the major ideas and main issues that emerge from the analysis of your qualitative data. Themes will be generated by the answers your participants have already provided and you'll discover them through analysis of those answers. Analysis will begin creating accurate transcriptions of what has been, and this will create textual data. Once you've done that, you'll begin the coding process and then move onto categorization. Through this process, regardless of whether your approach is inductive or deductive you'll discover meta-themes and potentially sub-themes that will allow you to fully answer your research question.

2

Section

Develop a relationship with your data through transcription

Q

How do I start looking for themes?

A

You start to look for themes by firstly organising your data into transcripts, the written versions of your data.

Creating accurate transcriptions is essential

Once you've audio recorded or filmed your participants answering your questions, it is crucially important to get what they have said into written form, this is called transcribing. Transcription will give you a detailed account of what was said by each participant, in each context, and this will allow you to begin your analysis: analysis that will ultimately lead to themes emerging that you can use to answer your research question and support your themes!

DO I HAVE TO TRANSCRIBE ALL OF MY RECORDINGS?

Transcribing all your data is essential. And the reason for this is that it:

- Enhances **familiarity** with what was said
- Enhances **accuracy** and precision in data presentation
- Allows for immediate **immersion** into your data
- Facilitates greater **understanding** of the phenomena being discussed
- Helps understand **contexts**
- Allows you to understand **idioms**
- Helps establish the **reliability** and **validity** of the research

CAN SOMEBODY ELSE DO IT?

Yes, potentially. **There are lots of available companies who will happily transcribe your data for you.** There are professional transcribers available (excellent, but potentially expensive), and online transcription services (relatively cheap and reasonably accurate) where you simply upload your file, either online or through an app, and transcriptions are produced within a day.

However, think carefully. **The more time you spend with your data, the better the relationship with it**, and in my experience a good relationship should start with personal transcription. However, it is undoubtedly a time-rich exercise, so it must be carefully considered against the time you have.

HOW TO GET STARTED

When beginning to transcribe it is of critical importance that you do so in a systematic way. Before you begin the transcription process, consider the following:

- Start each transcript with a list of those involved. This should be at the top of the page.
- Give each participant a code. This could be their name, or a pseudonym, but make sure to include their gender, participant number, and any information that makes them stand out (you'll need to know who they are, and it can be easily forgotten).
- Create margins on each side of the page that allow enough room for writing.

CREATING POWERFUL TRANSCRIPTIONS

Once you begin to transcribe **consider the following to ensure you maximize your time:**

- Double space every sentence. This will leave room for making notes, notes that will shape your codes, categories and themes.
- Give each line a number, this will you allow you to find extracts quickly and will help with comparisons.
- Don't try to type everything up in one go (breaks are essential).
- Type everything that is said. This includes bad language, pauses, repetition, stuttering, non-verbal nods, cultural references, when participants go off topic … everything!
- Be completely consistent doing the above. Shortcuts, no matter how tempting, will mean you may miss something.
- Plan regular breaks (essential) and reward yourself (vital).
- Read through the transcript while re-listening to the audio. You'll be surprised at what you've missed or mistakenly added.

TOP TIPS

1 Buy a recorder that has a button that will slow the audio down.

2 Time how long it takes you to do your first transcription. This will help you establish how long the whole process might take. Time management is key!

3 Use good headphones. If you block the world out, you'll get better transcripts.

4 Take lots of breaks (this is worth saying again).

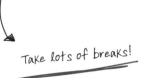

Take lots of breaks!

YOUR TRANSCRIPTION CHECKLIST

CHECKPOINT

- ☐ I know why I need to transcribe my recordings
- ☐ I know what approach to transcription I'm going to take
- ☐ I have the right equipment and materials to help me transcribe my recordings
- ☐ I know what company I'm going to contact to transcribe my recordings

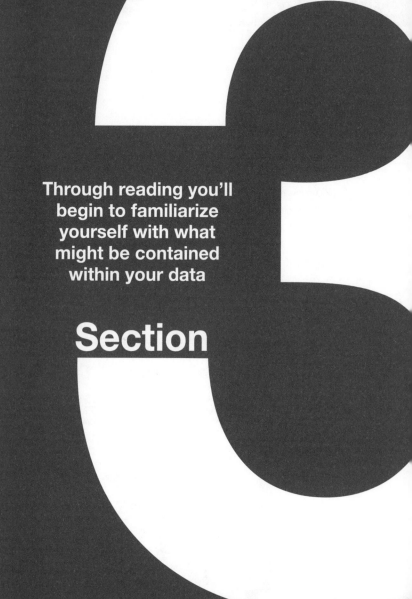

Through reading you'll begin to familiarize yourself with what might be contained within your data

Section 3

Q

What do I do with my transcripts?

A

You read them intently, diligently, and critically to ensure you develop a relationship with them.

The more you read, the more you know

How do you develop a relationship with your transcripts? The simple answer is to read them, but it's how you read them that counts. Reading a transcript should be thought of as diving into water. What happens when you dive into water? You're covered and fully immersed in it, and that's what we want from your reading. Don't dip your toe in and decide you don't like it. Get in, get accustomed to reading, stick with it and, for the few weeks you're involved, you'll find it's not as bad as you think.

DO I READ EVERTHING ALL AT ONCE?

You read one transcript at a time. **Never deal with more than one at a time.** This is the only way to really get to know the data, avoid assumptions and not miss something that might be significant.

WHAT IS THE POINT OF ALL THIS READING?

Through reading we become more familiar with what has been said, and **familiarization with what has been said by your participants enables you to start imposing a basic, analytic structure on the text** in relation to what has been said, why it has been said but, more importantly, what is the meaning of what has been said. Through this process you'll begin to think analytically and, more importantly, abstractly.

WHAT'S ABSTRACT THINKING AND HOW DO I DO IT?

Abstract thinking is thinking outside the box and about what the data might mean. When you're reading, try to avoid thinking literally, that's thinking about what's directly in front of you.

Ask yourself the following questions when you're reading to construct your own view on what the data means and think in an abstract way. That's exactly what we need to get to those themes!

- What is the participant's story? How did they get here? (you can impose some subjectivity into this.)

- What might have prompted them to say what they've said? (personal experience, opinion, influence from others, age, gender, generational issues.)

- What might be the implications of what has been said? (does the answer provide insight into future actions, behaviours, opinions or beliefs?)

- What are your own beliefs of what has been said? (your experiences can be invaluable in trying to decipher somebody else's.)

- What are your own interpretations of what has been said? (this is purely subjective, and really the essence of qualitative research.)

PRE-CODING

When you start reading make sure that you **use your notes from the interviews and start to highlight sections of text and sentences that might be of use.** This will allow you to start organising the data before we get into the main analytical stage.

We call this 'pre-coding', and it allows you to start making sense of your transcripts from the start. This is the beginning of the coding process and these simply need to be your initial thoughts and observations from the data collection process. No more than that.

WHAT'S THE BEST WAY TO PRE-CODE?

This is an important question and something lots of new researchers get wrong. You will start pre-coding by employing an approach that ensures you **read every line in a systematic and controlled way to get your thoughts down.** Some lines won't have relevance, but some will. Get used to this as you'll revisit this technique when you start coding more formally.

CHECKPOINT

TRUE/FALSE?

1 A simple scan reading of your transcripts is enough to get familiar with them.

- ☐ True
- ☐ False

2 You should read your transcripts all at the same time.

- ☐ True
- ☐ False

3 Concrete thinking is the ability to think about situations, experiences and events that may not be immediately present in the data.

- ☐ True
- ☐ False

CHECKPOINT

4 Abstract thinking is a thinking based on the facts and literal definitions found in the data.

- [ ] True
- [ ] False

5 Notes taken during interviews can help organize your transcripts.

- [ ] True
- [ ] False

6 Pre-coding can help you to start finding interesting elements in your transcripts.

- [ ] True
- [ ] False

Answers

1 False 2 False 3 False 4 False 5 True 6 True

CONGRATULATIONS!

You are ready to explore coding

#LittleQuickFix

4

Codes are the building blocks of your final themes

4 Section

Q

What’s a code?

A

You will need to make sure you are proficient with coding before you can start to organize and analyse your data.

What is coding and what are codes?

Coding is the first analytic step to establishing your themes and is described as the systematic process of generating phrases, sentences or key words that capture, summarize, or infer what you believe has been said by the participants in your research.

There are several ways to conduct and approach coding, but remember that first and foremost it is a personal journey, and there isn't one way to code. The codes you produce will have value, because you'll be the closest person to the data, and will understand it better than anybody else in these initial stages.

WHAT DOES CODING PRODUCE?

Coding will ultimately produce a series of codes. **Codes help you establish potential patterns in the text and should be viewed as the building blocks of what will become your themes.** Importantly then, your codes are not complete themes. But here's the payoff: good codes, will generate clear categories and clear categories will generate transparent and valid themes.

ARE THERE DIFFERENT APPROACHES TO CODING?

Yes. There are two distinct approaches to coding. These approaches are known as inductive and deductive. An inductive approach is theory building, and a deductive approach is theory testing. Essentially, are you finding something new, or are you establishing what is known? To make it clearer, have a look at the boxes below.

INDUCTIVE APPROACH

Coding and analysis stems from close reading of the data

Themes will emerge from the data

DEDUCTIVE APPROACH

Coding and analysis stems from what's already known in the literature

Themes will emerge from theory

We are not mutually exclusive

WHAT APPROACH SHOULD I USE?

The approach you employ will depend on your research question, but have another look at the boxes. The **approaches are not mutually exclusive, and the reality is, is that you'll end up applying a little bit of both**, because your participants may well provide new insight as well as conveying opinions, feelings and emotions that potentially conform to what is already known.

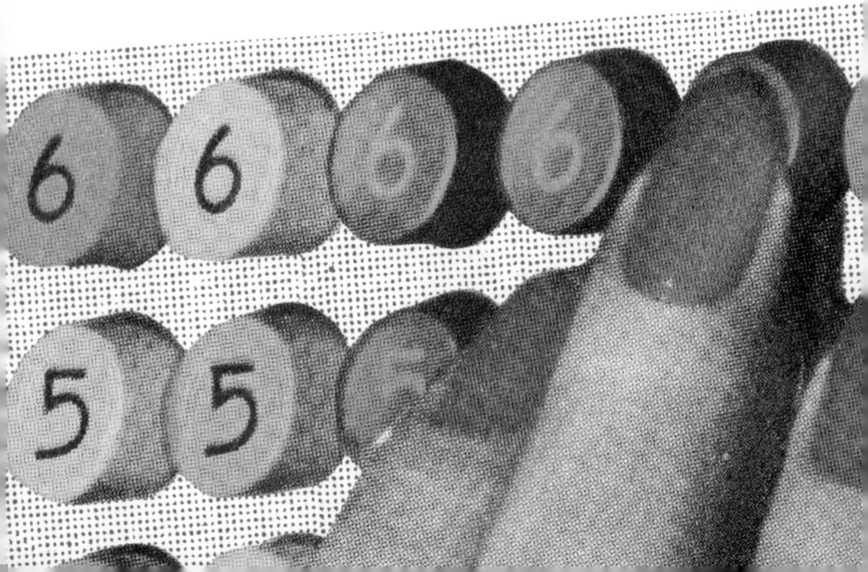

ARE THERE DIFFERENT WAYS TO CODE?

There are at least 25 ways to code, but don't be put off. **The practice is always the same: coding is about reducing your data.** But before you begin the process (we'll get to that in section 5), it's vitally important to distinguish between the two approaches (inductive and deductive) and the actual methods that can be employed to code.

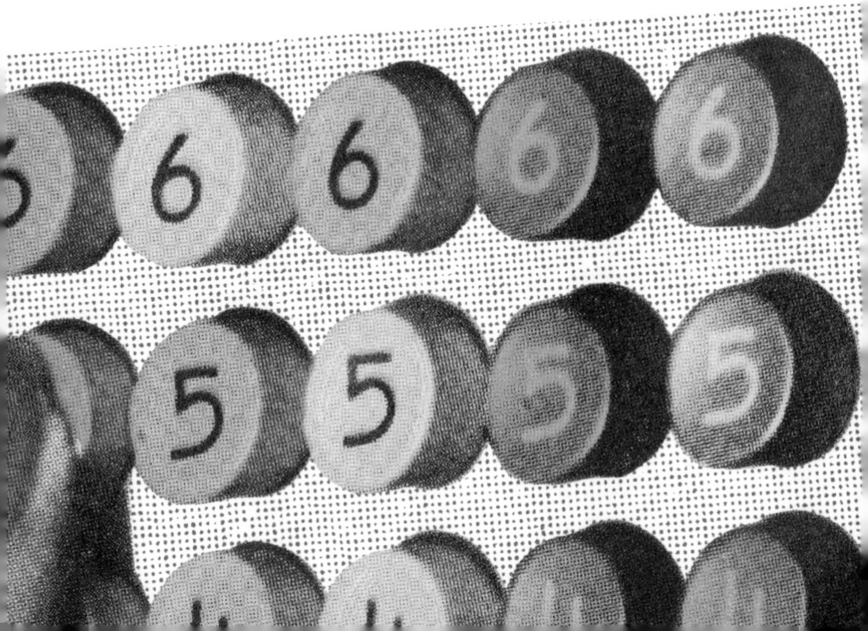

WHAT ARE THE DIFFERENT WAYS TO CODE?

Here are a few that you might find useful and should consider:

CODING METHOD	PURPOSE	BENEFIT	SUITABILITY
Emotional coding	Codes help reveal personal emotions	Helps understand human experience	Great if your work deals with human interactions
Versus coding	Codes help reveal tension between different groups	Helps the researcher understand different perceptions, feelings, and attitudes	Good for potential research where multiple groups are involved
Evaluation coding	Codes help reveal differing opinions over time	Can illuminate how attitudes evolve over time	Good for research that has multiple capture points
Verbal exchange coding	Codes help reveal interpersonal exchanges and their context	Can help identify the nature and dynamic of a distinct conversation	Useful for understanding interpersonal communication
Values coding	Codes help reveal personal values relating to a given subject	Helps identity individual perceptions of a given topic	Great for research that looks at culture

WHAT WAYS SHOULD I USE AS A STARTING POINT?

These approaches can be applied to any qualitative evaluation and are useful in capturing both specific and nonspecific elements in your data:

INITIAL CODING	DESCRIPTIVE CODING	IN VIVO CODING
Codes simply break down the text	Codes are summaries of what has been said	Codes are derived from exactly what has been said
Provides you with direction	This approach helps you identify what has been said	Significant phrases guide the coding process
This approach helps establish what data is immediately useful.	It helps you establish content.	This approach identifies 'stand-out' elements in your data.

WILL MY FIRST CODES BE MY ONLY CODES?

Probably not. **Multiple readings will lead to new insights, different ways of thinking, and potentially new codes.** You may even employ a different coding method. We call this 'second cycle coding' and it can help bring out more depth.

There is no superior way to code. All coding approaches pretty much borrow from each other, as they are all trying to do the same thing: find meaning and condense data.

TOP TIPS

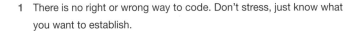

1 There is no right or wrong way to code. Don't stress, just know what you want to establish.

2 No approach is deemed better than another, so whatever you choose, just go for it.

3 Remember your recorder from your interviews? Yes? Good, use it to record your own thoughts regarding the data. This is useful!

CHECKPOINT

Get it?

Q: why are codes so important in qualitative research?

Got it!

A: because codes are the building blocks of the major themes that will represent the major ideas within a data set that support your research question.

Section 5

Codes represent the researcher's first attempts to make sense of their data

Q

How do I start to code?

A

Identify patterns in your transcripts by diving deeper into your data and reading your transcripts multiple

Your codes already exist in the text – you just have to find them

There are no shortcuts to generating codes, and to ensure you capture meaning and potential patterns in your data, you will need to spend lots of time with it. We covered reading in section 3, and you'll be aware that your relationship with the data is critical to developing familiarity, but this is where your reading becomes far more in-depth. Think of this approach as your search for evidence in the data, evidence that will allow you to begin to answer your research question. Your codes, generated through this probing approach, will capture and summarize this evidence and allow you to progress.

THINGS TO LOOK FOR IN EACH SENTENCE

When you start to look for meaning, remember it will already exist in what has been said by the participants. **Use the following list to locate potentially meaningful utterances** that will help you answer your research question and develop codes:

- Words/sentences/phrases that are repeated (a great starting point to build confidence)
- Words/sentences/phrases of general interest
- Words/sentences/phrases that are anomalous
- Words/sentences/phrases that are idiosyncratic
- Words/sentences/phrases that are expected or unexpected
- Words/sentences/phrases that are indigenous/cultural
- Pre-existing knowledge (this will come from theory)

WHAT SHOULD CODES CONSIST OF?

Ideally, **your codes should be short phrases that capture what has been said or convey what you feel the word, sentence or phrase points to.** They:

- Should be mutually exclusive (we don't want ambiguity)
- Should be independent (don't code a sentence as 'angry' and another sentence as 'angrier')
- Must be clear (this will help with the progression to categorization)
- Must capture a meaning (your code should reflect what something means)
- Must be multiple to ensure depth (this will help generate categories)

HOW MANY CODES WILL I NEED?

In this phase remember that you're pretty much separating the text into areas that you believe are important in the context of your research.

The **number of codes will depend on how much data you have and the nature and length of the transcripts.** There isn't a set amount, but filtering, re-reading, and greater familiarization can all impact on the number of codes you generate.

ASK FOR HELP

You can check the nature and validity of your codes by simply asking your supervisor, or an active research academic if they can go through them with you. This really is essential, and remember, your themes will take shape through your codes, so getting it right is important.

We call this intercoder reliability, and this process means that two (or potentially more) researchers should really agree on the codes and their meaning, with stronger agreement meaning stronger validity.

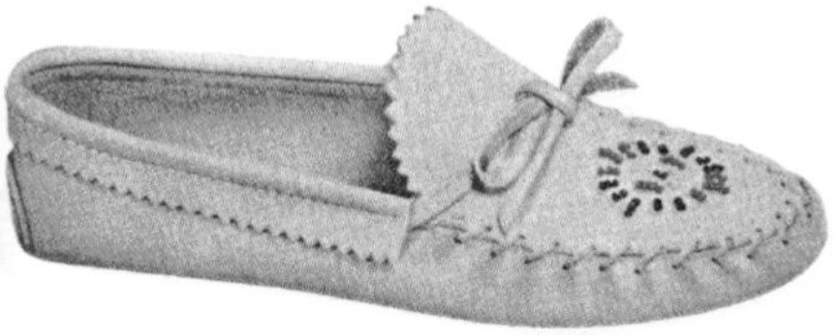

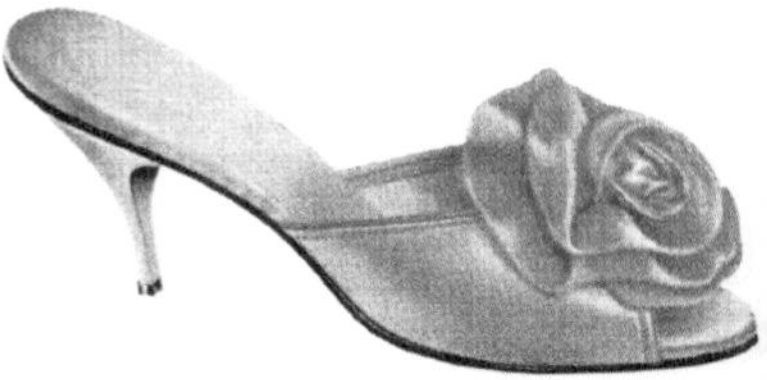

CAN A COMPUTER GENERATE CODES FOR ME?

There are lots of software packages available to help researchers. But the question is, are you proficient enough to use them? If the answer is no, then do this manually. If yes, then use an appropriate package to assist you.

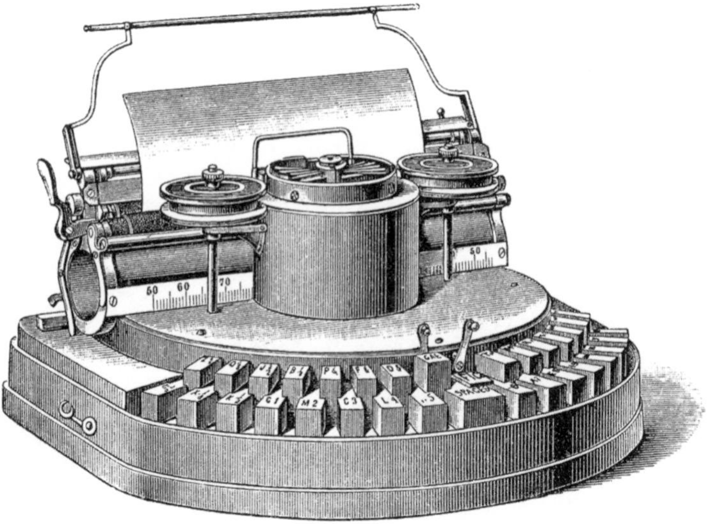

TOP TIPS

1 Use your research questions to help identity an initial direction.

2 Keep the question to hand throughout your coding.

3 Your codes may not be apparent on the first reading. This process takes time, so don't stress!

4 Codes are not an exact science; they are subjective, so have fun with them.

5 Make sure you develop codes properly; if you don't, you won't be able to compare the transcripts.

6 Keep a record of all your codes as you progress. They will change, and it's good to track these changes.

7 Good coding will help you identify what to keep in your study and what to reject in terms of your textual data.

DO IT YOURSELF

HOW TO DEVELOP CODES

Let's have a look at some data relating to the research question, 'how do millennials consume TV box sets?' The extract below is from participant 1 (P1). A 21 year old female student from a large family:

P1.

Oh, yea, I watched them on my own before I came to uni, but it isn't... the same, so it must be with my best friends; always with my best, verybest friends; we're all inclusive when it comes to box sets. So, to watch a set, I like to get everybody together, all my A-lister friends (laughs), and nobody else because I'm an A-lister (laughs). If we're all together, it's like we can speak about it, and that's like a LB [like back] on Instagram (laughter). If I don't do it like that, I don't get that, you know, chance to, umm, you know share the shocks, or discuss what's happened or what's going to happen. It must be with the right friends or it means I don't enjoy it as much.

Now use the following questions to help you find meaning in what you read, and generate codes that capture what you've found.

Remember, there's no right or wrong; just record what you see, think and feel. Be flexible and change your mind as often as you want, but once you're happy, check your thoughts with your supervisor to see if they found similar meaning.

1 Words/sentences/phrases that might be repeated

....

....

Possible code(s):

....

2 Words/sentences/phrases that you consider of general interest

....

....

Possible code(s):

....

3 Words/sentences/phrases that you think might be anomalous

Possible code(s):

4 Words/sentences/phrases that you think are idiosyncratic

Possible code(s):

5 Words/sentences/phrases that you feel are expected or unexpected

Possible code(s):

6 Words/sentences/phrases that might be indigenous/cultural

Possible code(s):

ANSWERS

1 'Friends', 'best friends', 'I'

Code – social significance/personal control

2 'I like to get everybody together, all my A-lister friends, nobody else'/ it must be with the right friends, or it means I don't enjoy it as much'

Code – exclusive activity.

3 'I'm an A-lister'

Code – acknowledgment/status

4 '…We're all inclusive when it comes to box sets'

Code – needs close interaction

5 'Oh, yea, I watched them on my own before I came to uni,'

Code – negative experience

6 'It's like a LB on instagram'

Code – needs recognition/positive emotions

CHECKPOINT

TEST YOURSELF!

Q: How are codes generated?

....

....

....

....

....

Answers

Through intensively reading the text, establishing key words, sentences and phrases, and then assigning meaning to them.

Section

6

Turn your codes into categories

Q

How do I turn my codes into categories?

A

summary

Through a process of comparing all your transcripts with one another, you'll begin to understand relationships between the texts; this process will turn your codes into categories.

What should categories do?

Your categories need to represent clearly identified and connected codes that share similarity in context and meaning, captured by an overarching word, phrase or short sentence that is representative of their shared characteristics.

Your categories need to be considered in the context of the information they contain, relate to, and represent. It needs to be clear. Don't take shortcuts. Categories bring your codes together and represent the penultimate analytical step!

HOW SHOULD I START THE CATEGORIZATION OF MY CODES?

Just like the codes, **categories are generated by you, and should help further condense your codes into more manageable, broader and more definitive chunks of data.**

Record your thoughts on what the code means to categorize effectively. If you do this, shared meaning and contexts will be far more apparent. To assist with this, create a table like the one below, which uses some of our data from section 5. Tables like this will help you see potential relationships more efficiently.

Question asked	Participant answer given	Code	Code meaning/ Researcher thinking
How do you like to watch box sets?	P1 'I like to get everybody together, all my A-lister friends, nobody else'	Exclusive activity	Evidence that watching box sets has a strong social context
	P1 '…we're all inclusive when it comes to box sets'	Highly personal interaction	Watching the box sets is about creating and strengthening friendships
	P1 '…and that's like a LB on Instagram'	Needs recognition/ positive emotions	Watching box sets together ensures reassuring interaction
	P1 'I'm an A-lister'	Acknowledgment/ Status	Social interaction ensures personal status

WHAT SHOULD MY CATEGORIES BE?

Like your codes, there isn't a hard or fast rule on the number of categories to include, and they can be named whatever you like. However, **they need to signify a distinct element that has been revealed through the coding process,** but in a far more specific manner than the codes themselves.

There isn't a special method for generating lots of categories; it's all through your ability to identify and see relationships within your codes.

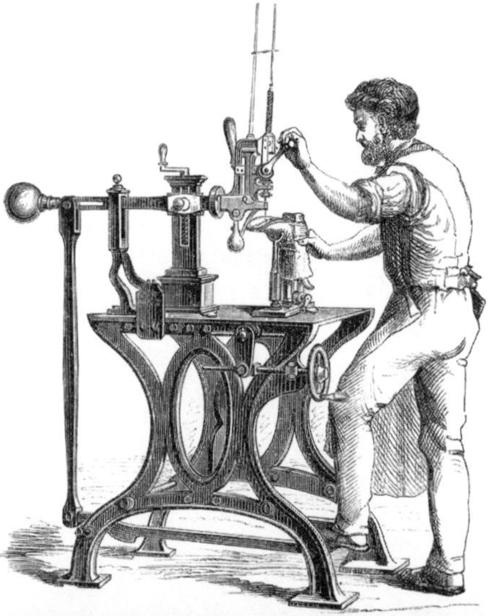

WHAT'S THE NEXT STEP?

Reassemble your data. **Map out your identified, similar codes so they're in front of you,** and do it for each question. If you're seeing similar answers to the same questions, and seeing similar codes across your transcripts, you may be onto something!

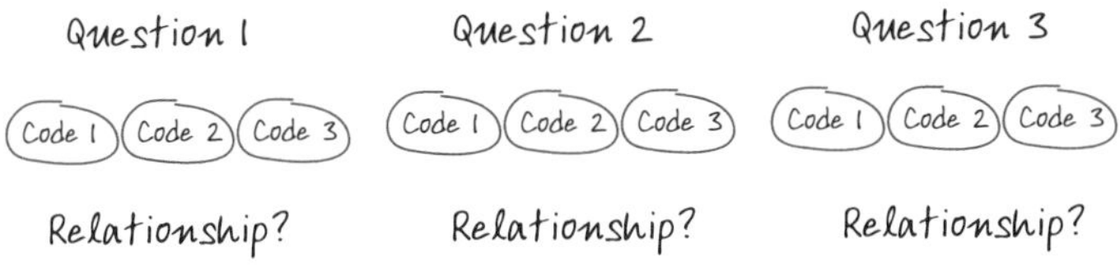

Several or indeed dozens of codes may have been produced, **and if you're seeing relationships, you're potentially seeing categories.** Great news!

DIDN'T YOU SAY SOMETHING ABOUT SUMMARIZING THE CODES?

That's right, we did. **A category is a way of summarizing several codes and therefore several pieces of your textual data.** Have a look at the visualisation below; it's all about relationships:

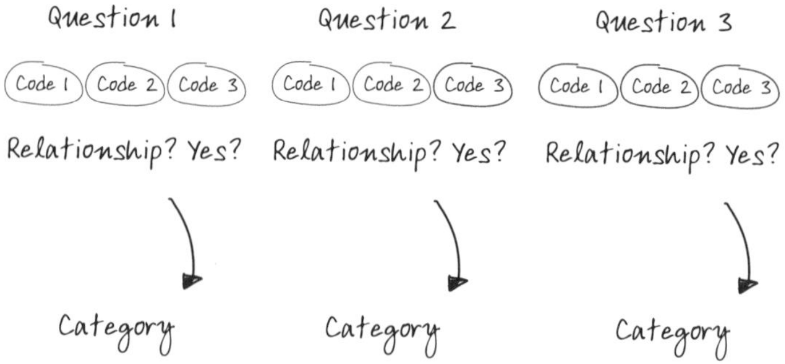

WHAT IF THERE ISN'T A CLEAR RELATIONSHIP BETWEEN SOME OF MY CODES?

This happens (a lot), so don't worry. If you have stand-alone codes, then simply put them to one side. Stand-alone codes, or codes without distinct frequency or immediate relationships may not form part of a broader category but can still be presented in your findings chapter to help answer your research question.

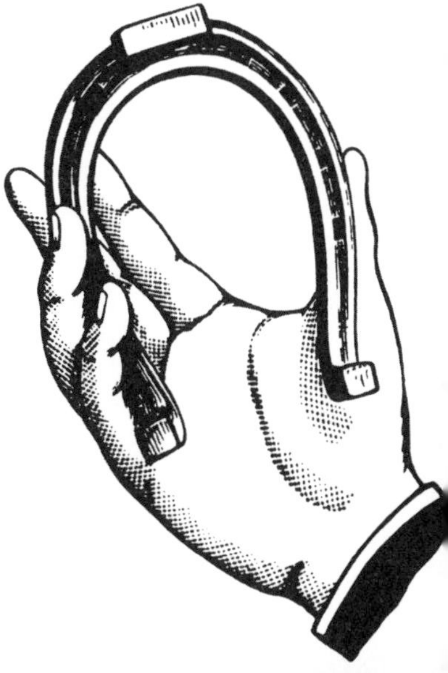

CHECKPOINT

CREATING CATEGORIES

Have a go at creating categories for the codes in the boxes. All you need to do is find a relationship, and a term that captures the overarching meaning of the connected codes.

Let's take the first one from the first table in this section. The question was: *how do you like to watch box sets?* Here are the codes from the first table in the section; can you provide a category that sums up those four, interconnected codes?

Exercise 1

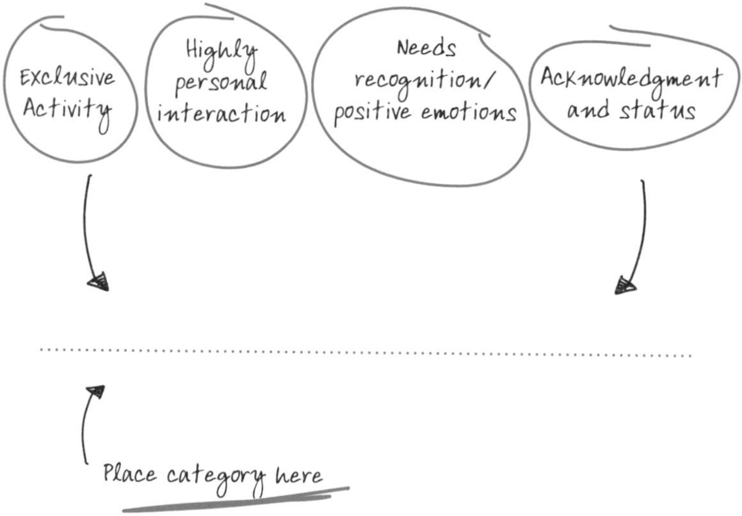

Exercise 2

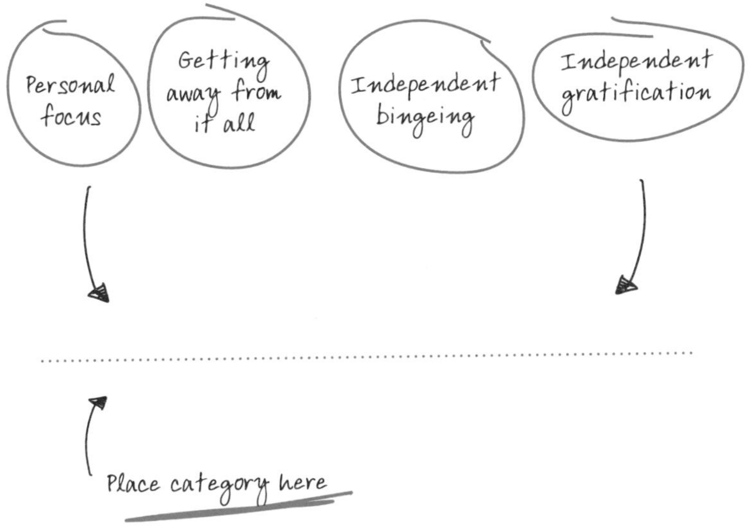

Answers: possible categories

Exercise 1: social authority; personal power; group control; individual influence; personal celebration; controlled collective experience.

Exercise 2: private experience; social escapism; individual enjoyment; need to unwind; watching what you want; avoiding interaction; quality time alone.

Once you've developed your categories you can start to develop themes

Section 7

Q

How do I turn my categories into themes?

A

10 SEC

summary

Once you have your categories, see if there are any distinct relationships between them that might represent significant concepts evident in your data set.

Condensing your data again

Turning categories into themes is purely a process of reduction. The important thing here is that you're not being asked to do anything new. You've already been through a similar process, so you're familiar with what the data is beginning to represent, but like coding and categorization, take your time, and change your mind as often as you want. Remember that your finalized themes should convey what's new, exciting, original, but most of all capture the elements that provide the answer to your research question.

ARE THEMES BASED ON MY CATEGORIES?

Yes. Themes are based on your categories, like your categories were based on your codes. So, again, it is about the relationship between the categories.

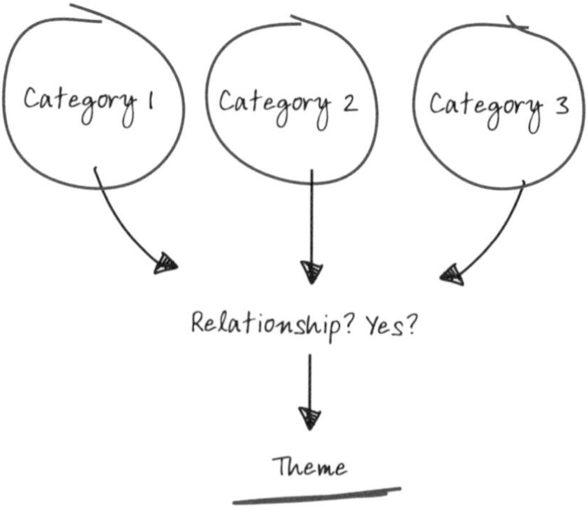

ARE THERE DIFFERENT TYPES OF THEMES?

Yes. You **may discover through the categories that you have several major themes or 'meta-themes' and several smaller, 'sub-themes'.** Combining both can help present the quality of what you've discovered in the data and help frame that all-important story line.

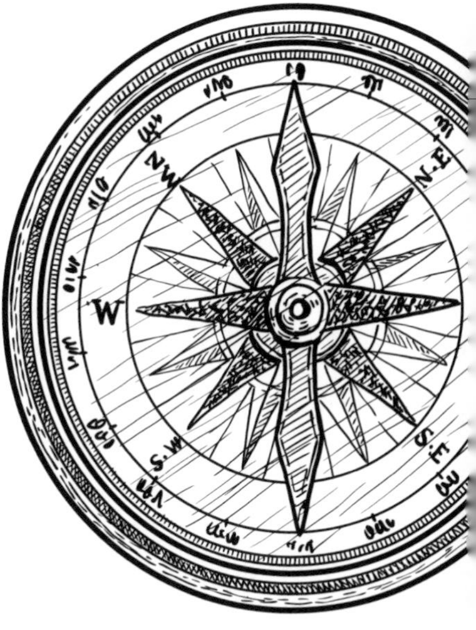

HOW DO I KNOW IF I HAVE A THEME?

A theme isn't a theme just because you say it is. Consider the following:

- ☐ Does the theme help me answer my research question? (This is arguably the most important consideration.)
- ☐ Have you identified meta or sub-themes? (Ask yourself if the type of textual data you're basing your themes on appears frequently, occasionally or intermittently.)
- ☐ Will your theme hold up to scrutiny? (Essentially, does your theme capture what you say it does?)
- ☐ Do your themes convey something insightful? (Do your themes accurately answer your research questions?)

HOW SHOULD I SUPPORT MY THEMES?

Your textual data will support and validate your meta-themes and potential sub-themes, and this will be presented in your findings chapter. It must be clear to the reader that your themes have emerged from your data. All your themes should be supported by evidence, so careful selection of the extracts you identified early in the process are essential. This basic model will help you make that connection:

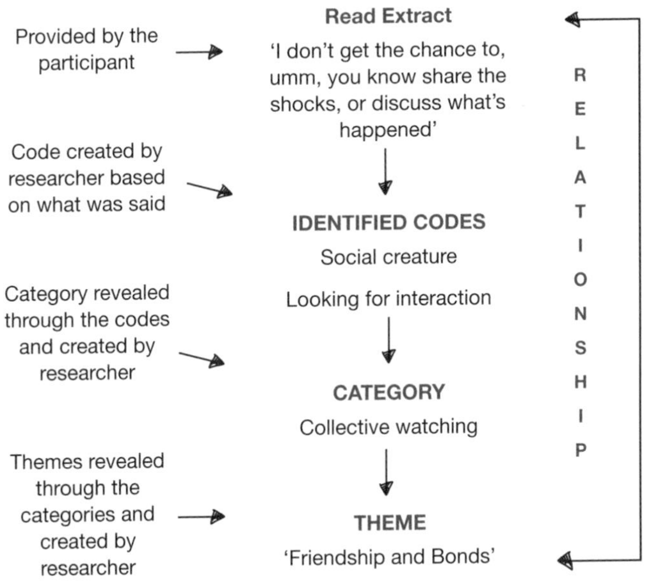
Read Extract
Provided by the participant
'I don't get the chance to, umm, you know share the shocks, or discuss what's happened'
Code created by researcher based on what was said
IDENTIFIED CODES
Social creature
Looking for interaction
Category revealed through the codes and created by researcher
CATEGORY
Collective watching
Themes revealed through the categories and created by researcher
THEME
'Friendship and Bonds'
RELATIONSHIP

HOW WILL I KNOW I HAVE ENOUGH THEMES?

Like many other questions regarding analysis, **there is no formula to indicate if you have enough themes.** If you stop finding them, then that's probably a fair indicator that you're done.

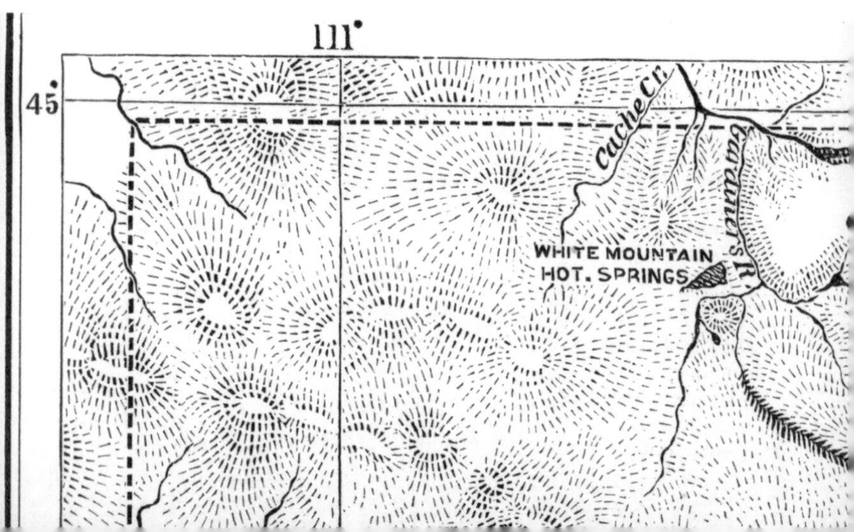

TOP TIPS

1 Don't rush into theme development. Take a break, revisit your categories, and you never know what you'll find when you go back.

2 Draw out a map like the one on p.105, you could even include it in your methodology to help with transparency (supervisors like that sort of thing).

3 The more you can demonstrate connections the better!

CHECKPOINT

MULTIPLE CHOICE QUESTIONS

Check your understanding with these questions:

1 In qualitative research a theme should represent?

- [ ] Your coding
- [ ] A central idea within the data
- [ ] What's been said
- [ ] What you know

2 What is a sub-theme?

- [ ] A type of code
- [ ] An interesting category
- [ ] A compatible idea with theory
- [ ] A secondary theme that supports a meta-theme

3 What should be used to support your theme?

- [ ] Your textual data
- [ ] Your supervisors' expertise
- [ ] Your codes
- [ ] Your categories

CHECKPOINT

CHECKPOINT

4 How many themes are appropriate for a thesis submission?

- ☐ 10
- ☐ 15
- ☐ 20
- ☐ There isn't a figure

5 What is a theme's major role?

- ☐ To demonstrate your data collection techniques
- ☐ To make your supervisor happy
- ☐ To answer your research question
- ☐ To show off your analysis

6 Where do your themes emerge from?

- ☐ Codes
- ☐ Categories
- ☐ Participants
- ☐ Data

Answers

1B 2D 3A 4D 5C 6B

Congratulations!

You know how to find themes in your data.

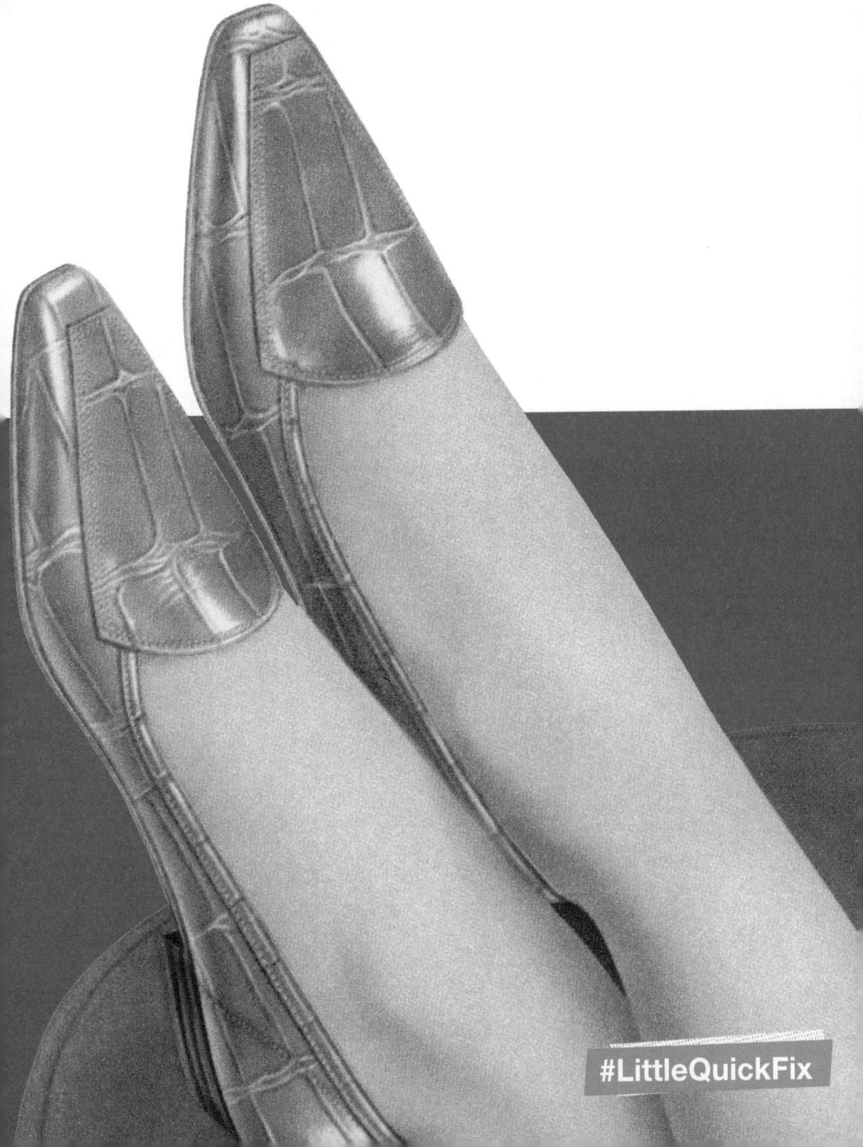
#LittleQuickFix

Ensure your themes are relevant, meaningful and representative

8

Section

Q

How will I know if my themes are meaningful?

A

This is perhaps where the subjectivity stops. You need to get a third party to evaluate whether or not your themes reflect the data.

Opinions matter

The only way to know if themes represent your proposed story line is to see if somebody else interprets the data in the same way. It is critical to get feedback, so don't be afraid to ask for it. But this process of validation starts with the research approach.

WHOSE OPINION SHOULD I GET?

Just like your codes and categories, use your supervisor or an academic researcher to verify your themes. Again, these individuals will have been on a similar journey and will provide an honest and supportive evaluation of your data.

It isn't common, but some research projects have used their participants to confirm what has been revealed in the data and to verify the authenticity of the themes.

TRANSPARENCY AND CREDIBILITY

Initially we need to take a small step backwards. Firstly, let's look at transparency. **Transparency relates to procedure in qualitative research, namely planning, execution, but naturally analysis well.** Is your analytical process clear from start to finish? If you can answer yes to this, your themes will be stronger for it.

Credibility relates to the whole research process. So, get clarity on your research rationale, philosophical stance, research design, methods employed and analysis. Like transparency, if there is a clearly defined and linear journey from data collection to data presentation, there won't be an issue. The reader will evaluate your themes like this, so bear that in mind.

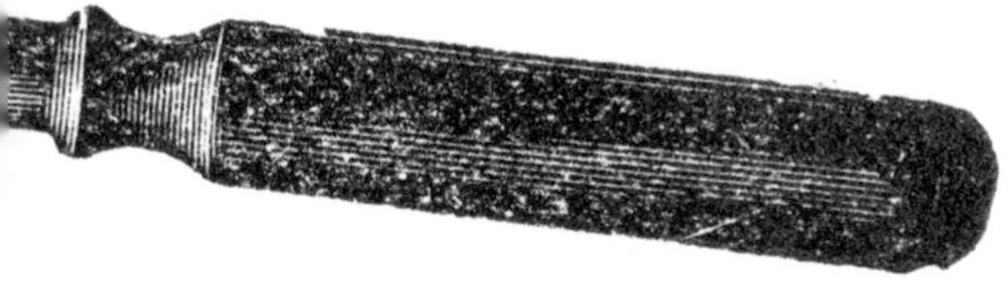

CONFIRMABILITY AND TRANSFERABILITY

Confirmability is the process of ensuring your findings are supported by the data you present. Sounds simple but remember you won't mark your own work. Qualitative research is subjective, but your interpretations need to be apparent to all. The good news is, if you've been reading this book, you will have been doing this from the start.

Transferability relates to the degrees to which your research result might be replicated in other situations. Essentially, a reader (marker) will ask if your data is a one off, or does it have greater depth and potential impact in other settings. To do this, make sure you sit with an academic to ensure the context of your research is upfront and clear, as clarity here will help tremendously in validating your research and final themes.

WILL THIS GIVE MY WORK VALIDITY?

It will certainly help. Validity in qualitative research is different to quantitative research. In quantitative research we use numbers and they cannot be interpreted: simply, 2 + 2 = 4, and that will never change, but what someone says can be open to different interpretation. So, in qualitative research, **validity can be established if your themes truly reflect what you believe they reflect.** If your themes are correct, your findings will be correct. So, get them checked!

TOP TIPS

1 Write your story out in full before you get an extra pair of eyes to look at it. The more complete the story, the more complete the feedback.

2 The clearer you can make your theme creation, the easier you make it for the reader to agree with you.

3 All qualitative research is open to scrutiny. It is unlikely that everybody will agree with your themes: so, relax!

HOW TO BUILD AUTHENTIC THEMES

DO IT YOURSELF

Use the following questions to ensure your work has transparency, credibility, and validity:

How will you ensure your work is constantly evaluated?

What will you do if your supervisor disagrees with some of your themes?

Who could you discuss your analysis with if your supervisor was unavailable?

What are the three main elements that need to be clear in your work to ensure transparency?

How will you ensure confirmability in your data?

BUILDING YOUR STORY

CHECKPOINT

Fill in this simple framework with your data to see how to build your story with your themes.

Story

↓

Beginning

↓

Middle

↓

End

THEME HEADING

....

....

THEME INTRODUCTION

....

....

DATA TO SUPPORT THEME

....

....

WHAT DOES THE EXTRACT REVEAL?

....

....

HOW DOES THIS ANSWER YOUR RESEACH QUESTION?

....

....

Congratulations!
You are ready to find the story in your data.

#LittleQuickFix

To make sure you master your data and get the full story from it, answer the following:

- ☐ Do you know what a theme is? If not go back to p.9
- ☐ Do you know the benefits of transcribing your data? If not, go back to p.26
- ☐ Have you understood the purpose of reading your transcripts multiple times? If not, go back to p.39
- ☐ Do you know what coding and codes are used for? If not, go back to p.54

HOW TO KNOW YOU ARE DONE

CHECKPOINT

- ☐ Do you know what to look for to start generating codes? If not, go back to p.70
- ☐ Do you know what your categories should represent? If not, go back to p.90
- ☐ Can you recall the difference between a meta-theme and a sub-theme? If not, go back to p.15
- ☐ Do you know how to see if your themes are authentic? If not, go back to p.118

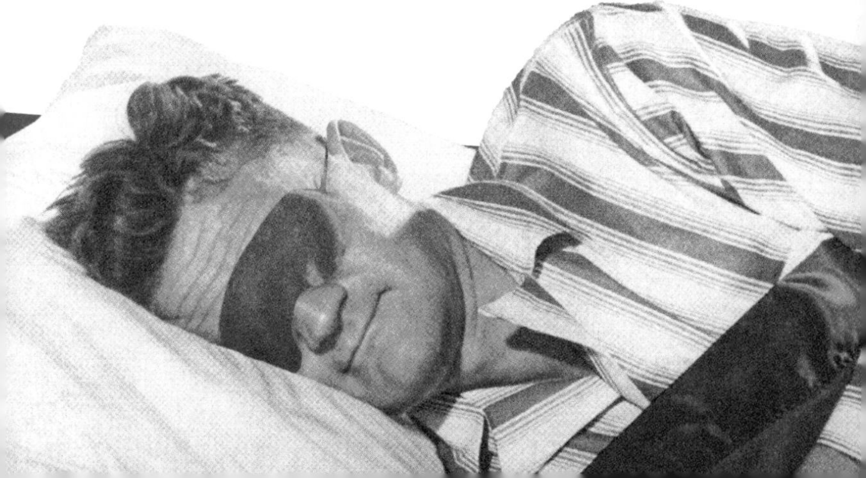

Glossary

Abstract thinking The ability to think about your data beyond what has simply been said by your participants. Looks to consider multiple meanings, not just what is present.

Ambiguity When a sentence, phrase or word may have more than one clear meaning.

Anomalous A sentence, act or behaviour that might be unexpected or unanticipated.

Category A type of classification in qualitative analysis that brings together several, similar codes.

Concrete thinking Literal, logical thinking that deals only with what is known. Considered the opposite to abstract thinking.

Code A basic building block of qualitative analysis.

Cultural An act, statement, word or behaviour that relates to a distinct culture.

Deductive When researchers use pre-determined ideas or pre-existing codes to help structure their data.

Emerge When an idea, concept or thought starts to become apparent or clearer.

Indigenous Relating to a behaviour, language or characteristic that can only be found or witnessed in a specific place.

Idiosyncratic A sentence, behaviour or act that might be considered unusual in terms of behavioural norms.

Inductive When the data itself is used to generate codes, categories and ultimately themes.

Qualitative research Exploratory research that captures personal opinions, thoughts and experiences.

Reliability Relates to the ways in which data is collected and what it represents.

Scrutiny A critical, in-depth evaluation of a piece of work.

Subjective Opinions or thoughts that are based on what you personally feel.

Textual data Data taken directly from what has been said.

Theme A topic revealed through analysis that enables the researcher to answer their question.

Transcription A written version of your data.